Blood Orange

Blood Orange

POEMS

Angela Narciso Torres (signature)

Angela Narciso Torres

Glenview Pub 32
Library
Apr. 12, 2014 (handwritten)

Willow Books, the Literary Division of Aquarius Press

Detroit, Michigan

Blood Orange

Editor: Randall Horton

Cover art: "Catalina" from the *Aura* series by Hermes Alegre. 48 x 36 oil on canvas. Courtesy of Charlie's Gallery collection, Bacolod City, Philippines.

Book cover design: Godfrey Carmona

Author photo: Rowie Torres

ISBN 978-0-9897357-2-8
LCCN 2013949041

Willow Books, a Division of Aquarius Press
PO Box 23096
Detroit, MI 48223
www.WillowLit.net

Printed in the United States of America

for Rowie, Matthew, Ian, and Tim

~

for Francisco and Carmen
who taught me the first songs

CONTENTS

I.

II.

III.

I

TO RETURN TO SAN JUAN

What ocean liner, which bus station
to the loam that bore the imprint
of my first patent leather shoes. How far
to the cogon grass that watched my shadow
lengthen to the frayed edges of day.
To know the gaggle of children
stoning mangoes on Pilar Street. To feel
the white heat of hand rhymes, mayflies,
a piano scale spiraling from a small window.
To enter the tile-roofed house, eyes smarting
from the sputter of onions in a blackened pot.
Awakened by rain on low eaves, to inhale
steaming pan de sal, the grainy crust soaked
in coffee—dark, smooth, then bitter
like a refrain one tries to forget. To hear
the soft slap of hemp slippers on stone
when evenings brought the smoke
of burning leaves.

There was always too much
to remember of San Juan—summer, a river,
stories the women sang. A shaft of light
igniting Tita Pacita's rooms at dusk.
The night Benny shot the Dizons' dog
with his BB gun, as it stretched on the carport
scratching fleas, only the tadpoles saw,
and none but stag beetles heard. And the bells
of Mary the Queen still pealed mornings
at seven, like the frogs returning after rain,
croaking their devotions to jasmine stars.

DARKROOM

Under the red lamp
I watch him douse
each small white square.

Side by side we search
the shallows, seafarers
peering through glass

for sliver of coast, rough ridge.
One by one he brings us
back—daughter, brother,

mother, son. Again and again
within light-tight walls
he births us.

Blood Mother

Two fingers on a pulse like the true point
of a divining rod, the almost-painless needle,
spring of crimson in a syringe—

the frailest patients sought her touch.
Peeling off nylons after rounds
she'd collapse into bed, hair sculpted

in its web of Aqua-net. Bathed and fed,
we sprawled on her bedroom floor
with homework, mapping the moonlit

country of her nearness. Her sleep
unbroken as chain stitches we practiced
in sewing class, interrupted only

by calls from the hospital—but not for
lost buttons, skinned knees. How could we
compete with a child pocked to the bone

with tumors, his hair razed by what saved him?
Monsoon to monsoon, we swallowed our questions
like puffs of air a balloon exhales before it bursts.

SOAP

Years later, my father would tell her
that while she was away
visiting family overseas,
the slowly shrinking soap
became a sacrament
of his loneliness,

and how, when he bathed on the eve
of my mother's return, the bar
had thinned to a petal
on the lip of the tub.

My Father's Rib

I was born with one rib
   missing. My father was
born with one too many.

Sometimes my fingers
   drift to the inch-wide gap
beneath my breast and I imagine

how my father must have felt
   his newborn for the missing
part. Did he wonder why a rib

and not a toe, a finger—
   an ear? Why this
curve of cartilage and bone,

one of twelve pairs
   guarding the pink
balloons of lungs, the liver,

the chambered heart?
   If my father
had the power then,

he'd have torn them—
   rib, skin, sinew,
flesh and all—

pressed it to the new
   life sleeping there
to close this cage of bones.

ARATILES

Little red moons, fragrant marbles pocketed, softening against my skin.

In the sharp grass behind grandmother's house, neighbor boys waited to grab the rubies from my skirt.

Thrives in poor soil. Not to be found in markets. Children thieve the berries from low-growing trees in backyards or sidewalks. Leave nothing to the birds.

In English: *Jamaican cherry. Panama berry.* In Malaysian: *Ceri kampung*, meaning; village cherry. In Spanish: *Cacaniqua. Bolaina yamanaza. Niguito. Memizo. Capulin.*

How names mean nothing till you've rolled them on your tongue, burst the juicy pulp against your palate.

Once, in Mexico, I glimpsed a basketful from the window of a taxi.

Aratiles. You can't say it without hearing rain on the roof of your mouth. Rain rattling the panes of an empty house.

On a boardwalk, a whiff of cotton candy on salt air brings back the grit of a hundred yellow seeds.

IRONING WOMAN

Afternoons I'd lie on her woven mat
of lemongrass and burnt leaves,
listening to tales of spurned love
on her bright-yellow transistor radio.
From her I learned what the old wives knew—

never to wash after ironing. Propelling
the gleaming prow across the ripples
of my father's shirt, she'd tell how the iron
gnarled her wrists, once smooth as bamboo.
How the steaming metal twisted
her veins, brought on "the shakes."
When I saw the serpentine rivers
on her arms, I knew this was true. Slowly

she'd raise both hands to show how
they trembled like maidenhair ferns
before a storm. Turning to her work,
her eyes reclaimed their stare
as though tracing a gull's shadow
over the surging sea.

56 Santo Tomas St.

Your patent shoes sink
in loam flecked with feathers,
seedcases split and empty. Already,
the summer frock you wear is short
for your four years. Knees frown
beneath the shirred skirt.

The black purse you clutch
was your sister's once. Your grasp
is tentative—you know some things
will never be wholly yours.

Your father lowers the lens,
asks you to move from the shade.
From the corner of your eye,
your grandmother, a grey-white
blur, shakes the bag of seed. You fix

your eyes beyond the camera.
The cage, a feathered
crescendo, ochre-green.
Your lit face
holds everything
as the shutter clicks.

ELEGY WITH ATLAS MOTH AND YELLOW BELLS

We may never see them again
   the giant-winged Lepidoptera
alighting on fire trees that shaded us
   at recess, our bench
a mass of knuckled roots.

About the size of a fruit bat,
   they spread their wings like burnt
maps across a span of leaves
   proving that beauty appears
to the small and lonely alike.

And it's unlikely that anyone will discover—
   as I did, leaning into a hollow bush
on the playground near the septic tank,
   the foliated room where sun poured
through yellow trumpet blooms

we could spy from our classroom.
   Daily we wrote in cursive to the swish
of Sister Angelica's skirts as she dusted
   a cracked row of encyclopedias,
June rain rinsing the window glass.

FREEDOM

The summer I turned eight, my brother let me slip
behind him on the glitter-blue seat of his bike, my arms
around his waist. In midday sun the pavement winked
like starlight. Wobbling into balance, we swerved past
the gate, leaving the chores, the barking of dogs, Yaya
on her siesta. The wheels burned, the wind made whips
of my hair. Down three blocks, the red-and-white striped
awning of Park Lane shaded its piles of fruit, candy
melting in jars, aspirin by the piece, sacks of rice,
ice cold drinks. And Rosemarie—storeowner, aging
movie star, wilting in curlers and kabuki make-up
behind the glass case of pencils, Band-Aids and glue.
In the air around her, the buzz of small children,
like bees to their queen. Her eyes, a shade lighter
than sorrow, widened with kindness when she called
in her lilting Filipino accent, *What do you like?* Faced
with the dilemma of Sarsi or Coke, I stood flamingo-
style, right foot on left leg, hand on hip, weighing
the heft of those minutes, the bondage
of indecision. Even the baby stopped crying.
The *tsk, tsk* of a lizard. From somewhere,
a love song on the radio.
                                Then oh, sweet
pop and hiss of the cap, the cold-bitter slap
of Coke streaking the back of my throat.
Oh, to be eight, to fly home on a bike
with your brother, belting out "Freedom"
like Aretha in the Blues Brothers, arms raised
to the heavens. On the sidewalk, our combined shadows
moved at the speed of clouds, the inky shape of
freedom, that twin-headed beast of terror and joy.

FUGUE

All she would remember when she woke
was how it began—the driver who bore her
through noonday traffic, his hand

never leaving the car horn, her fingers
tangled in her sister's, who earlier
in the schoolyard begged her

to walk faster, and she, knapsack in tow,
wondered why a horse galloped
in her chest or when it mattered

how slowly she moved, and why it was chill
in mid-June. And what was that look
on Mama's face, upon finding her slumped

against the door? Why did Mama slap
her hand? Could she have helped
how pale she was, how mottled

like a thrush's egg? They carried her
into the car then, made her lie down,
eyes reeling as the sky unfolded

like those scenes in home movies
when her father forgot to turn off
the camera, left it running in the back seat

so it captured birds on telephone wires,
someone leaning out a window, lampposts
that measured in yards the road

to the hospital where he worked,
the last frame before the city
guttered, went black.

WAITING FOR MY FATHER AT THE UNIVERSITY HOSPITAL LAB

On his desk, coiled against a fragment
of uterine wall, the fetus floated
in a Mason jar, pale thumb raised
to its voiceless straw of neck.
Shaken from mothballed sleep,
my father's lab coat—starched, pressed,
lily-white—sloped across his shoulders
behind the Underwood. A blank
sheet waited for letters to pound
through carbon: *malignant, benign,*
malignant, malignant, benign.

Pipette-thin, barely nine,
I crossed the doorway. No sound
but the shuffle of patent shoes on tile.
Clicking against the microscope,
his ice-cube lenses magnified
that other universe—berry-stained

cells congealed into rocks, ringlets,
ferns unfurled, moon craters.
Curled amid books and paper,
I became infinitesimal, a tight fist
of fire and constellations, no larger
than a dust mote on the camera lens
he polished with a scrap of chamois
before peering into the deep
rivers of a heart pinned open.

Elegy with Roller Skates

My hands in hers, she led me down
the pebbled path between our yards,
our shadows stammering out a waltz.

The way the gravel thrilled my calves
as I let go. And when I fell, how leaves,
or something darker, dimmed

her face. The way her bracelet caught
the sun when she bent down to fix
my straps, then pulled me up, my hands

in hers. From her I'd learn to slip
the metal snug around my shoes,
where to fit the key, and how

to fly. The last time I saw her,
she took my hands in hers the way
a dancer asks for one more dance

and then lets go.

MENARCHE

October cooled the kitchen where
Mother told how Father proposed
over a basket of *lanzones*, the tart-sweet
globes tumbling into her skirt and across
the floor. Pinching the brownish rind
till it split, I felt the first trickle,
sticky as sap on my fingers and chin.

A churning in my gut shot thin rods
of pain from unknown hollows. Air thick
with the cadence of Mother's voice, telling
the myth of this once poisonous tree.
A young woman—not mortal but a goddess,
the Virgin Mary, lost in the woods, searched
for a well to quench her baby's thirst.
From somewhere a branch offered its cluster
of bitter buds. Piercing the velvet hide
with a thumbnail, she cancelled the poison,
touched the nectar to his lips. The crying stilled.

With legs swinging, lips translucent
with sour-sweetness, my son now sits
on Mother's lap. I hear her tell again
the legend of *lanzones*. A plump orb slips
from the boy's hands; she peels it for him.
Dividing the flesh like a flower, five crescents
eclipsing the ghosts of pips, she points to
Mary's imprint on each segment, faint as a line
on her open palm. I choose from the basket,
this one, perfect, round, topped with
a small dark star, aureole of a nursing breast.

I press out the sap, take it with my tongue.
What comes back is not the strawberry stain
that bloomed like a rose on my cotton skirt,

not the words Mother spoke in the dim
of her room, but how I winced when I bit
into seed, acid infusing smoke-sweet pulp.

LUCKY

My mother looks for signs
on the morning of my departure.
Everything means something

else, she assures me when
I topple a juice glass,
calling it good fortune

when crystal shatters.
When I lose the coral
earrings she gave me

she blesses heaven—
Better that than your life.
So when she hears the flight's

been delayed—burnt fuse—
she's exultant, convinced
the gods have foiled some evil

design on my safety.
It delights her when
I call her from the gate

to say I've spilled
coffee on my favorite
sweater and yes, the weather

in Denver is fine. Mother
of contradictions, believer
in science and angels, for you

I'd stoop for the wayward pin,
avoid each sidewalk crack,
comb a field of wild clover—

to find you a balm for letting go.

II

THINGS TO TELL MY SON ABOUT THE MOON

She seemed so close, those October nights
on the bentwood rocker—her bright disc
rising at the wheel-shaped window

like the first face that greeted
your pale crescent of scalp before
its triumphant push into light. Then

I came to know the near perfect roundness
of your head, silver-downed, nestled
against my breast, taut with milk. Skin

to skin we watched the night pour out
from a ladle, tilted to spill the slow
spooling hours. In the silken silence

of a moth's cocoon, I listened for
the sound of your swallows, followed
the motions of your starfish hand, patting,

pulling loose a strand of my hair.
Somewhere I learned which cry meant
you had enough, or wanted more.

From spring to harvest moon I watched
the shadows move across your face,
explored new regions with borrowed light.

WE GO BACK TO MANILA IN 1999

What will our children remember
of the shape of that year? Perhaps
the city skyline, swathed in smog,
a plane landing at daybreak,

arms reaching to encircle their small
flight-weary bodies as they melted
into the waiting crowd. But those
were fleeting glimpses, through eyes

still fogged with sleep. More likely,
the sticky heat and stench of fumes,
a van weaving through early traffic
to the village that housed their mother's

memories, verdant still, a jungle-green
deeper than California's silver-sage.
Most certainly, the tile roof house where
they learned to call their grandparents

Lolo and *Lola*, learned to say *ulan* for rain;
rain filling potholes and gushing in gutters,
drumming on the low eaves, on windows
slammed shut to monsoon winds. Breakfast

of sweet sausage and rice, the clatter of pans
begun long before morning's hushed light,
punctuated by the calls of a bread vendor
peddling hot *pan de sal* on a bicycle.

Come Sunday—Mass, lunch, and
cousins, all honey-brown, coal eyes
shining with a primal fire they recognized;
a pilot flame igniting the ring of kinship,

amber like lamp-lit panes glazed with rain.
Older ones leading, they roamed the dark
rooms like a pack of wolves—
rummaging through cupboards and drawers,

prowling the backyard rubble to unearth
the stories from which they grew. In years
ahead, lulled by an electric fan's whirr,
their dreams will be peppered with the strange

names of fruit—*guava, caimito, siniguelas.*
The sudden sound of rain will rouse what's left
of distant, half-remembered trees: the heft
of rough branches, their slippery embrace.

SHEER

At the foot of her bed,
my mother, one knee pulled to her chest,
slipped nylon stockings over toes
then heel, releasing inch by inch
without hint of hesitation,
fine flesh-colored gauze she'd gathered
in her hands, stretching it smooth
over shaved skin. Never once
revealing a snag or tear.

Now from the top of the stairs
my teenage son glares unblinkingly,
the distance between us
straining like the skin of water
in a glass filled past the brim.
I can almost see how much I need
to learn about when to tug
and when to let go. How far
the net will hold before it rips.

Thursday, after Dinner at L'amie Donia

We arrive past midnight, stepping out of coats
and street shoes into the plum darkness
of stairs leading to our children's bedroom.
Through the railing of the top bunk,
our nine-year-old's limbs dangle, angular
and smooth as a sapling, his long bones
like bare branches in the sleep of winter,
the shy curve of biceps under a yellow sleeve.

Shirtless and coiled near the edge
of his mattress, our second lies cocooned
waist down in flannel, threadbare
from years of washing. His mouth is open,
his eyebrows, black feathers arranged
like question marks. I pull the quilt to his chin,
he murmurs—about what, I will never know.

Palms pressed together under a cheek,
the youngest rests on his side, one thigh
thrown over the balled-up sheet. At five years,
he spans the length of the toddler bed.
When I bend to lift his bangs, stringy with sweat,
the air fills with boy-smells: talc, sea-spray, metal.
His eyes scrunch together as if to seal out
moonlight. Standing in the room amid

three sleeping boys, their thin chests
swelling and emptying to different tempos,
I can almost believe they're mine to keep—
blood, bone, and breath, in that moment,
despite knowing what time has passed since
each slippery push that launched their drifting,
ineluctable as the movement of ships
or continents, away from where they started.

Other nights, after dining somewhere,
we could be reading in bed or making love
as they inch away, quiet as glaciers,
farther by the minute, fading like a dream I try
to describe in daylight. *Stay, stay*—I want to cry out,
but the images dim and blur at the edge of morning,
so that by noon I've lost entire stories, and starting
at the beginning doesn't help me to remember.

RITUAL

The winter sun
ages into brightness
in the small window
reflected in the mirror
where I sweep black
kohl over one eye,
and then the other.
Decades of mornings
practicing this as though
it were religion, and still
I have not perfected it.

Holding skin taut,
start with pencil tip
on inner corner of eyelid.
In one smooth motion,
staying close to lashes
as possible, draw a line
to lid's outer edge. End
with slight upward stroke.
Smudge. Repeat on other eye.

"Why are you doing that?"
my son asks. I look
in the mirror. The sun
has already left the window.

REFLECTION, 3 A.M.

The way the glow of a streetlamp
limned the blinds in my son's bedroom
where I'd stumbled half awake
to answer his fevered cry

and lying beside him on the narrow bed,
the way his feet burrowed like roots
into the lap they once pushed against
when he first wobbled upright,

brought back late afternoons
napping with my father, curtains drawn
to the green breath of trees,
thin light combed by blades of palm.
The way I hooked my ankle

to my father's leg so he wouldn't slip
away to his desk, his weekend chores,
believing a small foot sufficient
to anchor us, an axle on which
the vast afternoon slowly turned.

DIAGNOSIS

And the hour, the minute, that moment of knowing—
will it be on a day like this, the strong sun
glinting off tar in the hospital lot

so I forget where I parked my car,
or which way to turn when the zebra arm
unbars me after feeding the ticket stripe-side-down?

Will I fumble for the receiver when it rings,
or put on the sheath of composure? The calm
I learned at age five, looping my shoelaces

the way Mother taught me, muscle memory
taking over so I did it without thinking, what
enabled me this morning to pick up the phone

as I plowed through the interstate at rush hour?
Talking while driving, studies have shown,
is a matter of multitasking, I read now in *Time*

while waiting for the nurse to call my name.
A toggle in the brain, the neurons
switching tasks as a computer manages

multiple commands, fulfilling them in order
of what—ease? Urgency? The sequence in which
they were received? So which will come first—

numbness or fear—if the phone rings
while I'm peeling an onion, a toddler
at my hip, the kettle stifling a hiss?

FOR A SON TURNING SIXTEEN

By the time the black
   blade clears
my windshield—

   its *shush-thump*
the sound of blood amplified
   in a doctor's scope—

the roadside aspen,
   its windswept leaves spent
like so many coins,

   is gone. Before I can say
the last syllable
   of your name, you've bolted

through the back door,
   wheels crunching gravel
like small bones.

   And years ahead, when
I've emptied your drawer
   of photographs, plastered

the last under cellophane,
   your room will be light and dust,
books neat, shelves staggered

   by their heft. Whatever
bindings you left unbroken
   will stay unbroken,

what pages unturned,
   remain unturned,
dagger-edged, clean.

To Do

Call repairman about refrigerator gasket,
find model number first. Buy chicken-flavored
toothpaste for Lilli. Consult vet about lump
in her eyelid. Ask Jade if she can pick up Timmy from band.
Yoga class. Write Ian at camp. Search the basement
for Bishop's Collected Prose, re-read the piece about
her mother getting fitted for a purple dress in Nova Scotia.
Buy folder with metal prongs for Matt's book report. Schedule
the boys' dental check-ups, mammogram for me.
Write Irene about the boy with the faux-hawk and good
shoes on the train from Chicago, reading a Bible
from a zippered case. Tell about the elderly couple
and their two-year grandson, how the grandfather clutched
the boy when the train lurched, then picked him up
as though lifting a brittle Chinese urn from the mantle.
When the boy wriggled into his grandmother's lap, how she,
so unconcerned and vast, kept her eyes on her paperback,
held open with one hand, her other arm around the boy
who draped his body over her chest, his cheek on her padded
shoulder so he could look out the window. The grandfather
watched the boy with utter concentration, no—amazement—
at the small face, smooth as cream and lit from within,
watched him with the kind of awe for the young that only intensifies
as one grows older. How we grow older. I followed
the boy's sleepy gaze to the smokestacks, the skeletal trees,
the church spires, the leaning warehouses painted
with signs he could not yet read: Glass Block
Factory, Art's Body Shop, Bright Metals Finishing.

CROSS STITCH

At her son's ball game
under the shade of a straw hat
she works on the patch of irises
that she began seven years ago
to fill the long days before his birth.
Afternoons, she crossed squares on cloth
as on a calendar, stopping when
the pains shook her moist hands.

Lifting now the cream-white fabric
for the first time since he was born
she begins the needle's long-awaited return
along the edge of an unfurled leaf.
She remembers: the light of October,
how it lengthened on the starched square
that rested on her taut belly. A half pear
on the windowsill. The near-ripeness of waiting.

She fingers the strands of color—
gold leaf, sage, wine, cerise. Her eyes
trace patterns over empty rows
imposing on them the unfolding
of years. As though the stitches
might hold the shape of her firstborn
who reaches now, squinting in the outfield,
arms outstretched to the endless blue.

Things I Learned from My Sons While Driving Them Home from School

There is a religion in Vietnam that worships Charlie Chaplin and Victor Hugo.

Long Island has four McDonald's restaurants per square mile.

Mrs. Morris, the English teacher, swears.

In Dubai there is a group of islands arranged in the shape of a palm tree.

If you stand in the schoolyard at recess playing the Rocky theme on a kazoo, you could earn $1.27 and a refrigerator magnet.

All girls look better with bangs and makeup is the most disgusting invention ever.

You can't fold a paper in half more than eight times.

On the Baskin-Robbins logo, a pink 31, for thirty-one flavors, is hidden in the BR.

A boy in seventh grade breeds guppies in his locker and sells them in water bottles.

Imagine a ball of solid steel the size of the earth. A bird flies by and brushes its wing on the ball's surface once a year. When the entire ball has eroded, eternity is just beginning.

Driving My Mother to the Dentist I Learn of Her Fear of Umbrellas and Motorcycles

Umbrellas, because her pinky caught in one
once, in a typhoon. Motorcycles, ever since
her mother warned of the gap-toothed man
whose engine sputtered into town selling shiny
pots and pans, how he'd snatch her away
if she didn't finish her greens. A jeepney pours
carbon monoxide through our window.
We inch our way, she unravels

stories of the war, tells them as though
she were ten again, running through paddies
knee deep in mud and leeches, scattered
gunshot ringing the bowl of night. Huddled
in a shelter with her sisters, hunger's tooth
in her belly, she fell asleep to a squalling
newborn, a teaspoon scraping a tin
of powdered milk, the sweetest
never to pass her lips.

Now she is silent, she who was once
all music, fervor and fire, who can't recall
anything she had for breakfast, or whose
bright-eyed boy played at her feet
that morning. Beyond the traffic,
the cracked plains stretch to the hills.

FIRST DAY

Stopped at the red light, I see my son in line
with his classmates before the first bell, a boy
just twelve, slouched shoulders, easy smile
among the scrubbed Monday faces jostling
for space, bending to tie a shoe, rubbing sleep
from their eyes. And I don't know why
I expect him to find my car slowed in traffic
behind other parents rushing off to jobs,
to the store, to a sink full of dishes, coffee
and the paper in a quiet house, so when
he wheels around, his look unbalances me,
not exactly a smile, but maybe the beginning
of a smile, as when glancing sidelong
in the three-way mirror at a store,
that second of unfamiliarity, seeing *me*
and *not-me.* Like hearing a song
in a different key, the ear fooled
for a moment. The last time I saw my father,

Typhoon Talas shredded Manila's shantytowns,
floods rising to rooftops. The staircase to his room
creaked in new places, the doorknob twisted
too readily in my palm. In the mirror,
his snow-white hair, cheeks gaunt in the dim room,
the horn-rimmed glasses larger, darker
than I remember. But there was the same slope
of neck bent over a book. If I gathered
those hunched shoulders, if I shook them slightly
and asked, *when did everything change—*
what would he say? There's a story

my son made me read to him every night.
Three owlets wake in dark to find
their Owl Mother gone. *Perhaps she's
hunting,* the older ones say, *to get us food.*
But the youngest whimpers for his mother,

a plaintive refrain. Page after page of wanting
and waiting, until at last the Owl Mother comes.
Soft, silent, she swooped through the trees
to Sarah and Percy and Bill...

Relief, and something else, caught
in my voice before the story ended,
before my son sighed into his pillow. Leaving
my father at the airport, I felt that same charge
in the air when I turned from his embrace, unable
to meet his eyes and what was mirrored there.

Ahead, the light turns green, the bell rings,
schoolboys straighten their lines, wend their way
into the classroom. But I want to rewind
to that half-second before my son turned
his back, craning my neck as the traffic
begins to flow. Just then he waves,
as one day he will tilt his head, lift his palm
from a car or train, his hair burnished auburn
under a lit maple whose leaves have started
to rust, the sun barely warming the highest limbs.

III

Paris Aubade

Sunday. Sunlight from a white slit
where velvet drapes fail to meet
fingers the carved edge of a table,
your body curled in sleep like a child's,
thumb tucked in the cornucopia of your fist.

Could you blame me if the courtyard
rinsed by last night's rain pulled me
to my feet? Forgive me, but I am still
the daughter of my angry and beautiful mother,
impatient to turn the corner, to catch the first train.

How else would I remember the fruit
in the cobalt bowl this morning, the taste
already forgotten, but not its papered
globe, ripe and smooth as stone?
Physalis, the Sri Lankan waiter called it,

his teeth gleaming as he slipped me
the grocer's tag, knowing the sort of thing
travelers keep. Veiled in gray,
a nun hurries toward the sound of bells.
I follow her across the bridge to the shaft of sun
splicing two church spires as if to sever
its grandeur, the same light Matisse
would trail southward only to find
its intensity *superb, but terrifying.*

Sometimes I feel the vastness between us
even as we touch. But watching your face as you sleep
I can almost know you. As one knows the sky
from a swatch of white between parted curtains,
warmth from sun falling on a bowl of fruit.

BLOOD ORANGES

At the river's edge—
strewn seed, vermilion
petals from blood oranges

we ate. A branch
stoops from the weight
of phantom fruit. Falling,

the leaves exhale
the spice-heavy air,
its punishing sweet.

Entre Chien et Loup

More than tearing open the cream envelope
or hearing the shush of linen paper

between eager fingers, more than the rush
of ink-spattered words, there's the waiting—

or so romantics tell us, that expansive breath
held as if underwater for what seems forever,

each cell filled to bursting with oxygen—
for a lover's letter to arrive. Like that cold

January dreaming of your first kiss, lips
parted half-asleep in class or practicing

scales on the piano, something inside
ripens to almost breaking. Anyone

observing how magnolia buds flush
before they speak in white flame

will recognize the wish to linger
in airports or train stations, prolonging

that final glimpse, or the urge to pause
on a bridge watching dusk's vacillations.

Entre chien et loup, the French say,
implying that all we know of heaven

is the eyelash between day
and night, between dog and wolf.

Lost Objects

My mother-of-pearl pendant—
half a teardrop slung on a leather cord
bought from a hawker of veils
and batik. A brown book of poems

signed by the Indonesian poet
who sat next to me at dinner.
Four words remain in memory:
"To love, to wander…" I'm missing

a watercolor of vegetable vendors
given by my mother on the occasion
of my first apartment. The stillness
of those nights, the last box emptied,
searching the blank ceiling, imagining

the shades of green, the shapes
of the women—squatting, stooped, large
with child, bent over baskets piled with
a season's bounty. I'd give anything

to find my tape of Glenn Gould playing
Bach's Goldberg Variations, the one my father
copied for me on a gray cassette before the age
of compact discs. Hearing the first strains

at Mandrake Books on Story Street,
Mr. Rosen, my ninety-year-old boss,
paused at the window, lost
in shining sound, smooth as water
over stone. Idly he smiled,

arthritic knuckles tapping time
on a dog-eared Books-In-Print,
eyes fixed on some lost heaven.

POSTCARDS FROM BOHOL

1/

Emerald mounds rise from the deep,
their white shoulders shedding turquoise
waters. When we scoop the wet sand
fine putty sluices through our fingers.
Our heels sink inches with every step,
blurred footprints where small crabs
fine-pencil disappearing tracks.

2/

By dusk the tide has receded a hundred feet,
revealing the ribbed sea bed, ghost-pale
in the gathering dark. Scores of starfish
dot the rippled sand, white limbs etched
in gray, splayed under the night sky—
a universe in reverse. Ian, shirt flapping,
lifts a sun starfish, tentacles purpled,
radiating. We huddle around him,
our cheeks flushed with twilight.

3/

Driving through the country with windows
down, we count nipa huts, their thin walls
woven from palm fronds dark and light,
a diamond pattern framed in bamboo.
Dogs bark, a rooster tied to a gatepost scratches
and pecks, cocks its head. Children in faded
uniforms wave shyly, their feet red with dust.

BEETHOVEN'S MAID WRITES A LETTER TO HER MOTHER

His doctors have ordered fresh air and quiet
far from Vienna's crowded streets.
Barely a week since he arrived
and already the Master has broken
three plates. Yesterday he hurled a saucer
because the coffee was thin. *Thirty-two beans!*
he boomed. Picking violets for his tray,
I saw him at the window, head cocked
as one listening, ear pressed to a wall.

                      The pianoforte
roused me before dawn, crashing like a herd
of Lipizzaners, then soft and pleading
as Papi's face the day I left. When I brought
his breakfast, he wore a dressing gown, quill
in his hair. Music papered the floor. Mama,
at half-a-gulden a week, who knows when
I'll see you again? But this morning he paid me
twice my due. When I refused, he raised both hands,
saying, *I have no time to think of sums.*

Mornings he walks by the creek, papers
tucked in his arm. He notices neither heat
nor cold—wears linen in any weather.
Today at noon, beneath the cracked
elm I found him, fingers drumming
his knees, pages scattered like doves.
Nothing stirred. That's when he gripped
my arm, demanding, *Do you hear?*
Tell me, Anna—is that quail? Mama, I lied.

COLD FRONT

The whiff of clean laundry
   is not what I expect
at the door of Divine Word Seminary

   this morning, gray
slush sliding from my boots
   onto stone, but it takes away

the numbing chill to think
   of albs tumbling in a dryer,
warm suds swirling with wine,

   paraffin, human sweat.
Behind walls a monk folds
   chasubles, another sings

Tantum Ergo while swinging
   a chained thurible.
Incense infuses nave, linens,

   wood. Stooped on a pew,
a traveler might lift his eyes
   to the saturated reds and golds

of high windows, the lit robes
   of saints, plainchant
spiraling like smoke—

   might even be moved
to face the day differently,
   as I was, by the scent of clean

clothes. Outside, snow
   embroiders a veil on my window,
delicate as a girl's.

ISLA MUJERES

Waking up fevered in a foreign country, the bedclothes soaked,
my throat parched as a barren field, swatches of dreams float past,

like how I slinked behind an uncle at the Sunday table
to sip Coca-Cola from his glass, too timid to ask my grandmother

for my own. The sound of my voice croaking *Invictus* to great-aunts
nodding on the couch had me willing my nine-year body to vanish like smoke.

Back from Japan, my mother made me pick between two faux-silk robes.
I coveted the jade with cherry blossoms but convinced myself it looked better

on my sister's fairer skin. Do certain trees feel less, or more, entitled to
their patch of dirt and air? Do we ever outgrow childhood? And do scapulars

really save, like the two-faced medallion wedged into the sidewalk—Christ's bleeding
heart on one side, Immaculate Mary on the other? In a dark alley, my friend Melissa

clutched hers while praying "Mother Mary, may those who see me
be reminded," and the man with the knife left her. Lying in half-light, an iron vise

clamping my gut, even my hand is unfamiliar and everyone I know has gone fishing.
I can pretend to believe almost anything, even the efficacy of a pendant

embedded in my neck. I try to pray, but all that comes is a string of Spanish
memorized on the train and the first lines of *Padre Nuestro*. Repeat

what you know, a teacher once said, and the rest will follow. I intone it like a mantra—
Hagase tu voluntad, Thy will be done—but all that returns is the sea's roar

like drowned names of towns we crossed in the night.

MISSING

Like Carnaval screams, the two o'clock train
rends the blue night in half since you've gone to Brazil.

Minas Gerais, Maranhao, Curritiba, Contagem—
my litany of sorrows since you've gone to Brazil.

The grass is a woman's unpinned hair. *Bom Dia*,
cry the zinnias, since you've gone to Brazil.

The dishwasher rattles, the neighbors complain. The radio
stammers like Amazon rain since you've gone to Brazil.

Could the *Sonnets from the Portuguese* cool this
burning on my tongue since you've gone to Brazil?

Squirrels nest in the lilac where your hedger
hasn't sputtered since you've gone to Brazil.

I've baked enough bread to scatter to the crows.
I've knit you an ocean since you've gone to Brazil.

XCARET

Riviera Maya, Mexico

The sign says thirty minutes
to the river. Backpacks
like boulders, hiking boots

chafing in thick heat, we turn
away from the jungle's mouth
when a ranger calls out,

Don't think it too much!
It's meditation, he winks,
his slicked back hair

the bluish black of grackles,
one palm spread to a path
half-choked by thorns.

We lower our heads
to overhanging vines,
spider monkeys' cries and split-

tailed birds, one foot trailing
the other through the jungle's
deep vein, a seething tunnel

where time is a garter
snake that expands
and contracts. Don't think it

too much? we repeat.
We check our watches.
It's hard to see the sun,

hemmed by giant ferns.
Slapping at gnats,
we grunt uphill.

Don't. Think
it. Too much—
we heave, worrying

the words like wood
beads polished
to a high shine. Somewhere

the trail dips. Gravity
pulls us forward.
The canteen trickles

dry. Our breath
tumbles ahead of us.
Like pebbles, we spill

from the forest's arteries
to a river trilling light
down to its stony depths.

SAMPAGUITA

Sampaguita, a variety of jasmine that blooms at night, is the Philippines' national flower.

The full sun does not singe
our five-petaled faces.
Nestled in the deep
gloss of leaves, we only
bloom more fiercely.

By night, our long-fingered
scent goes to your head.
But seeds? We have none.
Cut off our roots—
we multiply faster.

So we do not mind
when children pluck
our tender buds, sew them
into wreaths for the dust-
rimed necks of your saints.

When you kneel down
to pray, our perfume will encircle
your brow. You'll remember
how a girl, barefoot and empty-
bellied, tapped on the glass

of your air-conditioned car,
traded a rosary of whorled petals
for the change in your pocket.
And if on equatorial nights
we open our mouths

as if to sing, what we mean
to say is, you may not
find us in the morning
unless the wind has dropped
our withered tunics in your path.

SONG OF THE SEA WITH THREE LINES FROM CARLOS DRUMMOND DE ANDRADE

Why does the deep seem deeper, the sea
wilder this morning? Next to it, life
is a static sun without warmth or light.
Our backs, not bent over desks, uncoil.
Lungs fill with air. Freed from leather,
our feet leave disappearing shapes
on the wave-swept bed. *Friendships, birthdays,*
personal matters don't count. Everything is relative,

says my uncle, lying half-blind on his sickbed
near a window so he can hear the ocean.
The breeze carries salt and decaying fish.
Unable to eat, he sips lemongrass tea, dreams
of garlic rice. *Don't sing about your city, leave it*
in peace, he says, then asks to hear calypso.

Night Jasmine

Years after in the dark, in the heat
of summer, through parted curtains it came
in search of me, the scent of night-blooming
jasmine from a windswept porch.

The girls who pierced white buds
into leis were long gone, the painted
swing seat rusted and worn
where mothers snapped sweet peas
over a game of cards.

How long the day seemed, how little
we knew of what our mothers hoped
to forget, their cares kept hidden
like coins we buried in the vacant lot.

What song played on the lime green
phonograph, underwater sounds that rippled
in widening circles to the waning afternoon,
through cracks in our hiding places?

Like smoke from clove cigarettes
or the silk of someone's fingers on my wrist—
you're found, come home—the song
unwound its spool, repeating
how far we'd gone.

ACKNOWLEDGMENTS

I am deeply grateful to the editors of the following publications in which versions of these poems have appeared:

Another & Another: An Anthology from the Grind Daily Writing Series: "Sampaguita"; "Things I Learned from My Sons While Driving Them Home from School"

Babaylan Speaks: "Ironing Woman"; "We Go Back to Manila in 1999"

Baltimore Review: "Waiting for My Father at the University Hospital Lab"

Cimarron Review: "Ritual"

Collagist: "My Father's Rib"; "Things I Learned from My Sons While Driving Them Home from School"

Colorado Review: "Missing"

Crab Orchard Review: "Menarche"; "To Return to San Juan"

Cream City Review: "Entre Chien et Loup"

DMQ Review: "Isla Mujeres"

Drunken Boat: "Song of the Sea with Three Lines from Carlos Drummond de Andrade"

A Face to Meet the Faces: An Anthology of Contemporary Persona Poetry: "Beethoven's Maid Writes a Letter to her Mother"

Going Home to a Landscape: Writings by Filipinas (Calyx, 2003): "We Go Back to Manila in 1999"

Hanggang Sa Muli: Homecoming Stories for the Filipino Soul: "To Return to San Juan"

HerMark 2009: "Paris Aubade"

MahMag: "Driving My Mother to the Dentist I Learn of Her Fear of Umbrellas and Motorcycles"

North American Review: "Blood Oranges"; "Cross Stitch"; "Things to Tell My Son about the Moon"; "Thursday, After Dinner at L'amie Donia" (received 2nd place in NAR's James Hearst Poetry Prize 2004)

Rattle: "Postcards from Bohol"

Sand Hill Review: "Elegy with Roller Skates"; "Freedom"; "Fugue"; "Night Jasmine"; "Soap"; "Reflection, 3 A.M."

Seven Corners: "Lost Objects"; "56 Santo Tomas Street"; "Darkroom"; "Elegy with Atlas Moth and Yellow Bells"

Stealing Time Magazine: "For a Son Turning Sixteen"

YARN: "To Do"

For their untiring support for underrepresented writers, for their generosity and guidance, and for making this book a reality, my deepest gratitude to Heather Buchanan, Randall Horton, and the staff at Willow Books/Aquarius Press. For gifts of time, space, and resources, huge thanks to Ragdale Foundation, Midwest Writing Center, and Illinois Arts Council. For reviewing this manuscript with patience, rigor, and kindness, I am grateful to Virginia Bell, Joanne Diaz, Ralph Hamilton, and Joan Houlihan. For reading these poems with eyes, heart, and soul, I thank Karen Llagas and Reine Marie Bonnie Melvin. For their mentorship and belief in my work, endless thanks to the faculty at Warren Wilson MFA Program for Writers, especially Jennifer Grotz, Brooks Haxton, Daniel Tobin, Ellen Bryant Voigt, and C. Dale Young. For invaluable support, encouragement, and friendship, my warmest appreciation goes to my co-editors at *RHINO*, my second family. And finally, for being my home, my inspiration, and the heart pulsing through these poems, all my love and gratitude to Rowie, Matthew, Ian, Tim, Kit, Menchi, and Lourdes.

ABOUT THE AUTHOR

Angela Narciso Torres is the winner of the Willow Books Literature Award for Poetry. Recent work appears in *Cimarron Review, Colorado Review,* and *Cream City Review.* A graduate of Warren Wilson MFA Program for Writers and the Harvard Graduate School of Education, Angela has received fellowships from the Illinois Arts Council, Ragdale Foundation, and Midwest Writing Center. Born in Brooklyn and raised in Manila, she currently resides in Chicago, where she teaches poetry workshops and serves as a senior poetry editor for *RHINO.*